Chinese Culture

Active Learning Series - #8

China's Foods

Developed by
Dr. Jane Liedtke - OCDF Publications

Published by
OCDF Publications, a division of Our Chinese Daughters Foundation

Endorsed by
Huáng Yǒuyì 黄友义, Vice President of China International Publishing Group and the Translators Association of China
Lín Wùsūn 林戊荪, Retired President of CIPG, Senior Editor & Translator

Contributors, Authors, and Editors:

Dr. Jane Liedtke, OCDF Publications CEO and Founder
Sharon Nakhimovsky, OCDF Publications Editor
Suí Hóng 隋宏, OCDF Publications Project Manager of Explore-A-Province Series
Sūn Xiǎobīng 孙小兵, OCDF Publications Editor
Megan Zaroda, OCDF Publications Project Manager of Chinese Culture Active Learning Series and China's Foods Author

A special thanks to the chefs at Tiān Wài Tiān 天外天 restaurant in Běijīng 北京 for providing supplies, hands-on instruction, and recipes from their kitchen for this book.

ISBN-13: 978-1-934487-08-2
ISBN-10: 1-934487-08-2

© Copyright 2009 - All rights reserved by OCDF Publications. Single classroom and single event use permitted only for purchaser of book. International rights reserved.

Contents   Page

Teacher Introduction and Planning Strategies	1-2
Bulletin Board Resources and Ideas	3
Class Discussion Topics, Projects, and Assignments	4-5
Approaches to Active Learning*	6
Student Information Sheets*	7-24
Student Recipes*	25-28
References and Resources	29
OCDF Publications Support Materials and Supplies	inside front cover
About OCDF Publications	inside back cover
Order Information	back cover

CDRom Features

In addition to pdf files of the above information, the CDRom with this book includes:
- Inside Chinese Restaurants
  - Interview with Chef Zhōng 钟 from Tiān Wài Tiān 天外天 in Běijīng 北京
  - Behind-the-Scenes Photos
- Additional Student Recipes of China's Foods
- Story-telling in English & Mandarin with Handouts in English/Chinese & Pīnyīn 拼音
- Additional Student Handouts* for China's Foods
- Additional Student Activities* for China's Foods
- Puzzles
- Images of China's Foods
- Teacher Tips - Ideas, Charts, Resources

* Reproducible for single classroom use or single event with maximum of 30 children.

i

Teacher Introduction and Planning Strategies

China's Foods

A common greeting in China is "Have you eaten?" or "Nǐ chīfàn le ma? 你吃饭了吗?" This is because eating is such an important part of life in China. Since China is one of the world's largest countries and is home to one fifth of the world's population, you can just imagine the variety of ingredients, cooking methods, and dishes available. What you eat from your local Chinese takeout is just a tiny fraction of what you can taste in China!

Chinese food can be classified by the "Eight Great Traditions," or eight main regional cuisines. These include the foods of Ānhuī 安徽, Guǎngdōng 广东, Fújiàn 福建, Húnán 湖南, Jiāngsū 江苏, Shāndōng 山东, Sìchuān 四川, and Zhèjiāng 浙江. However, it is becoming increasingly common to identify foods by geographical regions (east, west, north, south) even though there are differences in local food traditions in those four areas. In this book, Chinese cuisine is divided into these four regions versus the Eight Traditions.

Distinctive regional flavors and styles can be seen in the dishes themselves, but there is not as much difference in ingredients. This is because regions often share the same ingredients. What changes is the amount used in each dish. However, not all ingredients are the same because a region's food uses ingredients that are cheap and easy to grow in that region. For example, rice grows best in a warm, moist climate, so rice is the staple food in southern China. The cold, dry north is more hospitable to hardier plants like wheat and barley.

The Daoist philosopher Lǎo Zǐ 老子 said that governing a country is much like cooking a small fish. While cooking a fish may seem like a simple task, it is much more complex. A chef needs to select the freshest fish, understand how it needs to be prepared, know what, how much of, and when to add seasonings – all before the fish even gets cooked! What Lǎo Zǐ meant by his statement is that both cooking and ruling are deceivingly simple tasks.

This is very true of Chinese cooking. Chinese chefs pride themselves on using the freshest ingredients, mastering the finest knife skills, and perfecting the art of timing in their cooking. One Chinese food essayist wrote that a country's food is a guide to its culture. Tasty cuisine reflects a people's genius in invention, skill and patience in preparation, and knowledge of how to make life pleasurable. If that theory holds any weight, then the Chinese have a very rich culture indeed.

Metric Measurement
When referring to the metric system of measurement, the international conventions and spellings will be used.

Key Symbols in the Active Learning Series:
Use a **CD Boom Box** to play CDRom music or use a **microcomputer** to listen to a story or do an assignment online.

CDRom with instructional materials and handouts. Grab a **pencil or pen** to complete an assignment.

Take a **field trip** from school or prepare to **cook** some Chinese food! Or, prepare **activity supplies** in advance.

Reading Tips!

When there are Chinese words in the text, it may prove challenging for some teachers/parents unfamiliar with the language. Either use the CDRom where the text has been provided with narration by a native Chinese speaker or locate a Chinese speaker to read to your class. In this way, the teacher/parent facilitates the class, but does not have to worry about getting the Chinese words correct. It is important for children to hear the Chinese words spoken with the proper pronunciation and tones. If you do plan to read it yourself, please check with a native Chinese speaker so you can practice speaking with the correct tones. Stories are provided in audio with Mandarin and written form with English, Pīnyīn 拼音 and simplified Chinese characters.

Language Differences:

Please note that the official language in the People's Republic of China is **Mandarin** (Pǔtōnghuà 普通话). Many people throughout the country speak other regional languages or dialects, and may have accents. In southern China in Guǎngzhōu 广州 and Hong Kong, Cantonese is widely spoken. The written language using simplified characters is the same throughout the country no matter what spoken dialect is used. For the island of Táiwān 台湾, traditional Chinese characters are used for writing and Mandarin is spoken, but may not conform entirely to the Mandarin used throughout China. Throughout our books and materials, spoken Chinese will be Mandarin and written Chinese will be **simplified characters**. The Romanized phonetic version of the characters will be **Pīnyīn** (versus Wade Giles used in Táiwān).

© Copyright 2009 - All rights reserved by OCDF Publications. Single classroom and single event use permitted for purchaser of this book.

Grades	Stories/Activities about China's Foods	Student Materials

PreK-K
Teacher develops displays and bulletin boards
Teacher reads to students about China's Foods and shows images/photos from CDRom
Chinese person invited to the classroom to share about the regional Chinese foods they know
Teacher plans an activity from the selection of information sheets and activities on CDRom
Students complete a hands-on activity related to   Teacher follows activity sheet
    China's Foods   Teacher obtains supplies/materials

1-3
Teacher develops displays and bulletin boards related to the China's Foods
Teacher reads to students about China's Foods and shows images/photos from CDRom
Chinese person invited to the classroom to share about the regional Chinese foods they know
Teacher plans an activity from the selection of information sheets and activities on CDRom
Students complete a hands-on activity related to   Teacher follows activity sheet
    China's Foods   Teacher obtains supplies/materials
Class invites a Chinese association/group to present about China's Foods
Class has a guest chef visit to cook lunch with them or demonstrate cooking techniques

4-5
Students develop displays and bulletin boards related to China's Foods
Students read story about China's Foods and view images/photos from CDRom
                                                    Teacher copies student handouts
Chinese person invited to the classroom to share about the regional Chinese foods they know
Students complete a hands-on activity related to   Teacher copies activity sheets
    China's Foods   Teacher obtains supplies/materials
Class invites a Chinese association/group to present about China's Foods
Class has a guest chef visit to cook lunch with them or demonstrate cooking techniques

6-8
Students develop displays and bulletin boards related to China's Foods
Students read information sheets about regional cuisines of China and view images/photos from
    CDRom   Teacher copies student handouts
Chinese person invited to the classroom to share about the regional Chinese foods they know
Students complete a hands-on activity related to   Teacher copies activity sheets
    China's Foods   Teacher obtains supplies/materials
Class invites a Chinese association/group/parents to present about China's Foods
Class has a guest chef visit to cook lunch with them or demonstrate cooking techniques
Students work in teams to prepare presentations about the cuisines of China and their
    characteristics

Culture and Heritage Day Events
    Parent show CDRom images of China to group   Parent copies student handouts
    Children do hands-on activity related to China's Foods   Parent copies student activities
        Parent obtains supplies/materials
    Children discuss cuisines of China, create a menu, and then visit a Chinese restaurant
        to try the foods
    Children use large map of China to identify food characteristics of the provinces where
        they are originally from   Parent brings food-related
    Use foods from local restaurant in a taste-test   information about the provinces
    Cooking class for older children/teens   of children who will attend the
        function

Bulletin Board Resources and Ideas

Border Ideas for Bulletin Boards:

1. Alternate the names of yīn 阴 and yáng 阳 foods along the border of your bulletin board. Yīn foods can be written in blue since they are "cooling" foods and yáng foods can be written in red.
2. Line the bulletin board with chopsticks. Cut a bowl shape out of a piece of construction paper and glue grains of rice to it. Put these bowls in the corners of the board.
3. Print photos of Chinese dishes or ingredients and attach them to the edges of the board.
4. Glue tea bags to the vertical sides of the bulletin board and create paper tea cups to sit in the lower corners.
5. Line the bulletin board with recipe cards and write the name of a Chinese dish on each.

Bulletin Board Ideas:

1. Try the 100 dishes of Empress Dowager activity and staple paper plates to the board. Let children cut out pictures of food, glue or tape the food to each plate, and identify which dishes they'd include in a Chinese banquet.
2. Flatten Chinese takeout containers and staple them to the board. On each one, write a different Chinese dish. Include some that students know and enjoy and others that they don't know or might not like. Ask them to identify which foods they would take home.
3. Draw a large yīn-yáng symbol on the board and have students fill in yīn and yáng foods on the appropriate sides. Compare this overall Chinese diet to the western food pyramid.
4. Create a large dining room table on the bulletin board. Cut construction paper into squares to represent chairs, circles to represent people, and triangles to represent table settings. Have students set the table and seat people in the appropriate places based on Chinese banquet customs and dining etiquette.
5. Divide the board into five sections and label them "salty," "sweet," "bitter," "sour," and "spicy." List different foods, drinks, or spices that fall into each category. Staple pictures that correspond to the categories as well.
6. Obtain a large map of China (available from OCDF Publications) to serve as the focal point for the display. First mark the food regions, then identify the spices, grains, meats, and agriculture commonly found in those areas. This can be extended by connecting famous dishes from the region to those ingredients.
7. Divide the board into two columns - one for the price of food in China and the other for the price of food in your country. Attach the containers for a few food items such as milk or cereal to the board and have students guess the prices of the items.
8. Learn about food words in Chinese. Using information from the book and the CDRom, copy the names and characters for common meats, vegetables, fruits, cooking terms, and traditional dishes in Mandarin Chinese. Chinese characters began as pictographs, or pictures that represent an idea. Over time, they changed into the simplified versions they are today. Can you still see or can you imagine how these characters look like the food? For example, notice that the character for beef looks like a steer (niú 牛) or that the character for house (jiā 家) is a pig with a roof over its head.
9. Create a three-dimensional food display. Use modeling clay or paper mache to create various dishes on paper plates. Color them with paint or markers, and label the foods. Attach the paper plates to the bulletin board. You can focus on food groups or regional foods, and then link these foods to regions on a map of China.

© Copyright 2009 - All rights reserved by OCDF Publications. Single classroom and single event use permitted for purchaser of this book.

Class Discussion Topics and Projects

Discussion Ideas
1. Learning about China's Foods with Chinese People
   a. Which Chinese foods do we like? What about them do we want to learn more about?
   b. Who can help us learn more about the regional foods of China? Where can we find someone who has knowledge about Chinese food and would be willing to share it with us? Can we find them in the business, retiree, or restaurant communities or among the faculty of a college or school? Do we have any Chinese neighbors who might be able to help us? A restaurateur or professor of food and nutrition from a local college or university would be a perfect guest speaker on this topic.
   c. Where can we find resources that will help us learn more about the regional foods of China we like? Is there a Chinese culture center, Chinese learning center or institute or a Chinatown nearby? How will we get there? What will it cost to go there? How long will it take?
   d. What do we hope to learn from these experiences? What questions do we want to ask our new friends? To what events might we want to invite our new friends?
   e. What would it be like to taste the regional foods while in China? What would it be like to eat breakfast, lunch, snack, and dinner in China?

2. Learning about China's Foods in the Classroom
   a. How can we continue to learn from our Chinese friends we met outside the classroom? Can we invite them to come speak to our class? Can we organize a program or festival and include them? Can we ask them for recommendations on recipes, movies, books, and web sites that will help us continue to learn about Chinese foods? What gifts can we buy to show them our gratitude?
   b. What dishes do my classmates and teachers like? Which Chinese foods do they like the most? Do they agree with me or not? Why or why not?

Themed Projects or Events
Exploring China's Foods

In-school or community-based programs are ways to study various Chinese foods. Try these options or brainstorm with your students to see what ideas they may have!

1. Create a China's Foods cook-off. Ask cooks from a local Chinese restaurant, Chinese neighbors, or anyone who's talented in the kitchen to prepare a dish from a regional cuisine. You can either use the recipes from this book or encourage chefs to find/use their own! Divide the classroom or dining hall into five stations: one for northern Chinese food, southern, eastern, western, and minority foods. Invite students from other classes and parents to try new Chinese foods and vote for their favorites!

2. Get permission from school staff to use the cafeteria during a non-lunch time. Invite a chef from a Chinese restaurant to show students how to prepare ingredients for a dish, such as cutting meats, slicing vegetables, and dicing spices. Create an opportunity for the students to work hands-on with the chef to make a Chinese meal for their classmates.

3. During the students' lunch hour, arrange classroom or cafeteria tables as if students were attending a Chinese banquet. Prepare or order Chinese food, or allow students to bring their own lunches. Follow terms of banquet etiquette such as waiting for the host to eat before eating yourself, making toasts, etc.

4. If there is a doctor practicing traditional Chinese medicine or food therapy in your area, arrange for him or her to speak to the class and do simple analyses of their body types and yīn-yáng 阴阳 diets.

5. Create a mural showing various foods of China. Use a large vinyl version of the map of China, and then use water-soluble markers to draw the topography, regional foods, etc. on the map.

6. Obtain cookbooks from all over the world - Europe, Africa, South America, etc. Compare the familiar with the unfamiliar to learn more about Chinese cooking. How do the countries' land size, topography, climate, and population affect the types of foods that are grown and eaten?

© Copyright 2009 - All rights reserved by OCDF Publications. Single classroom and single event use permitted for purchaser of this book.

Assignments

1. Look at the menu in your local Chinese restaurant or browse the shelves of the Asian section of your grocery store. How many of the dishes or products seem authentically Chinese? What area of China do these dishes come from? In which cuisine are the ingredients used most often?
2. Tell your friends and family about some traditional Chinese dining manners and practice using them at your own dinner table.
3. Chinese foods can have symbolic meanings. What about the foods your family eats? Research the foods you eat or those of your ethnicity. Do they have symbolic meanings? If so, what do they mean and why do they have those meanings?
4. Try making a Chinese dish at home using the recipes included in this book or on the CDRom.
5. Look at the main ingredients in some of your favorite foods and those in Chinese dishes. What is the same and what is different? How can the same ingredients taste differently in different dishes?
6. There are many additional handouts related to Chinese cuisine provided on the CDRom. Use these as in-class or take-home assignments.
7. There are images related to Chinese cuisine on the CDRom. Use these images to design a visual menu for an imaginary restaurant you are about to open. Alternatively, make a Chinese cuisine resource guide. Locate places in your community where you can purchase chopsticks, spices, ingredients, and Chinese cooking supplies. Compile these into a guide for classroom families or visiting Asian families.

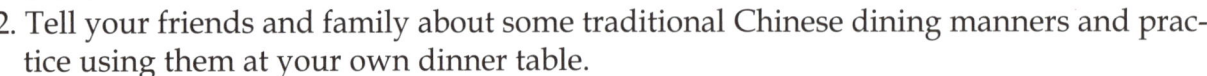

Research Projects and Activities for Older Students or Gifted/Talented Classes:

1. Create a timeline indicating when foods were discovered, when foods were brought to China, and when cooking methods or tools originated in China. Compare the dates to those in the history of foods and cooking in other countries.
2. The origin of both the noodle and the dumpling has been debated for many, many years. China claims to have invented both, but Italy and Russia also say they invented these foods. Research what archaeologists and historians have to say about the debate and make a case for the country you believe to have been the inventor of the foods.
3. Research two of China's biggest food exports, rice and tea, and track how they've influenced other countries and how widely accepted those products have become. Also, what are the rules and laws in China related to the import and export of food? How does that affect people's daily lives? What food products produced near your home end up in China?
4. A country's cuisines can be divided by region. Do a regional study of the food in your country. What flavors or cooking styles are common to the different geographical regions?
5. Chinese dining etiquette is quite different from that in many Western cultures. How have dining customs changed in your country over the years? What might be some reasons for the change?
6. How has the migration of farmers to the cities impacted the production of food products (such as vegetables, grains, fruits) in China?
7. How are Chinese chefs trained to cook Chinese food? Is it similar or different than learning to cook western-style foods? What special training is required for specialty dishes like Peking duck?
8. How have people adapted the style and design of their kitchens in China to reflect regional and local foods?
9. Create charts to depict the positive and negative actions of people relative to the environment in China and their impact on food production.

© Copyright 2009 - All rights reserved by OCDF Publications. Single classroom and single event use permitted for purchaser of this book.

Approaches to Active Learning!

To the Teacher/Parent:
When designing instruction and selecting activities related to your objectives, remember that learning about Chinese culture is not extra-curricular nor extra-mural. Chinese culture learning (from knowledge to activities) can be part of a broad-based curriculum in the humanities and social sciences, or part of language arts-related instruction or second-language instruction. Teachers can use Chinese culture activities to reinforce mathematics, science, and technology units of study. Even in physical education we can use Chinese culture as a means to try new physical activities (take tai chi, dragon and lion dancing, and dragon boating as examples).

Therefore, when selecting topics for the study of China's Foods, do not limit your thinking as a teacher/parent/homeschooler to - "How can we learn about the famous dishes of China?" Go a step or two further! This is why we have loaded the CDRom with many student activties, teacher tips, and ideas for how to examine the cultural practices of China with students. We'll leave it up to you to adjust for differences in age and language ability. We want to be sure you, as the teacher/parent gain the ideas and background information necessary to make good choices and explore Chinese culture with your students.

Instructional Design Elements to Remember:
Complete an analysis of various aspects of Chinese culture - what aspects of Chinese culture related to China's Foods do students who are at the grade level you are targeting need to know? Learning should be fun! Students should explore outside their normal comfort zones in order to change their perspectives and grow in their understanding of other cultures. Likewise, students should be engaging in activities that mirror real life whether that be real life from a historical perspective or real life from a contemporary perspective. Honesty and reality are essential.

Students learn best when they are learning in the cognitive, psychomotor, and affective domains (See Mager, *Preparing Instructional Objectives*). Create units of instruction that pull together many learning strategies and approaches to insure that this can happen. Try to teach to all three domains! This task should be easy with Chinese Culture Active Learning Series!

Authentic Assessment is Key! Evaluate the abilities of students in "real-world" contexts. In other words, students learn how to apply their skills to real tasks and projects (such as crafts and arts, music and dance, applications of technology, etc). Authentic assessment focuses students as ACTIVE participants in their learning. Of great importance will be students' analytical skills, ability to integrate what they learn with other subjects, creativity, ability to work collaboratively, and written and oral expression skills. It values the learning process as much as the finished product.

In authentic assessment, students engage in Active Learning!
Students plan events and activities - outings, programs, performances, celebrations, contests, etc.
Students conduct research and write stories and reports. They can keep journals and prepare portfolios.
Students read and interpret literature and use that as a base to create other activities or outcomes.
Students solve problems in new ways by applying mathematics, science, and technology to real-world issues.

Why authentic assessment? When learning about Chinese culture, it makes little sense to approach student evaluation through testing, memorization, or traditional Q&A. For students to be successful in a global society, their skill sets must be transferrable and demonstrated through critical thinking as well as using values-driven problem solving.

How can I use authentic assessment in my classroom? First, start with thematic units of instruction that use a range of instructional strategies. Activities where students engage in writing/rewriting, presentations, analysis, debate/disucssion, and teaming promotes learning cooperatively. When that process is in place, traditional testing makes no sense! Use short investigations to check student progress and have portfolios where student progress is visual - teacher, students and parents can see progress. And do not neglect the role of the student/learner in assessment. Engage and involve students in their own assessment of learning. This adds another layer of learning and possibilities!

© Copyright 2009 - All rights reserved by OCDF Publications. Single classroom and single event use permitted for purchaser of this book.

Student Information Sheet

Student Name _____   Class/Grade Level _____ Date _____

Chinese Banquets and Dining Etiquette

According to legend, when the Qīng 清 Emperor Kāngxī 康熙 was asked to repair and rebuild the Great Wall to defend China from enemies in the north, he had a different idea. If he kept his enemies' stomachs happy, they would not want to attack. Instead of fighting, he would treat his enemies to large meals called banquets. He also married his daughters to northern Mongols so that the two groups would be both in-laws and allies. He held many banquets in the Mongol territory, but very few Mongols ever came to Běijīng 北京. This was because there was a very contagious disease in the north that he didn't want people in the capital city to get. However, he thought the Mongols deserved a banquet in an imperial setting, so he built a palace in Chéngdé 承德, which was four hours north of Běijīng. The

banquets there were second in importance only to the one held for the Emperor's birthday!

Banquets during the Míng 明 (1368-1644) and Qīng (1616-1911) dynasties were elaborate and could have up to 400 courses! There were also many formal rituals that had to be followed. For example, guests would have to kowtow, or bow on one knee, to the emperor. There were so many rituals that by the time guests got to the meal, it was cold!

Banquets Today

Today's banquets aren't as formal or as elaborate, but they are still a very important part of Chinese culture. They can be held for business deals, special family events like weddings, or for holidays. Tables are round and seat eight to 12 people. People must sit in specific places and follow rules for how you need to eat. If you were at a Chinese banquet, where would you be sitting? Find out by reading the text box on the opposite page.

The number of dishes at a banquet varies, but there will be at least one more dish than the number of people sitting at the table. There is always an even number of dishes. Cold dishes and appetizers come first, followed by vegetables. A very decorative meat dish will arrive, followed by other meats, and soup is also served to help people digest their food. The last dish is a fish served whole because it is considered lucky. Rice and noodle dishes will end the meal. In restaurants, the food is placed on a Lazy Susan (spinning table) in the middle of the table so that guests can easily reach all of the dishes. Guests are served by the person to their right.

An important part of banquets is making toasts. The host makes the first toast and is followed by family members and guests. People hold their glass in the air and wish good luck or fortune. Guests should always toast with the same glass as the host. This means that if the host picks up a glass of juice or wine, the guest should also pick up the same drink.

Feast of Land Delicacies and Game

This is a sample menu from a Manchu-Hàn 汉 banquet held in 1764. At this banquet, 320 courses were served and 124 of them were pastries! Each guest had their place set with pink porcelain.

Cakes and dumplings: Peach, canary, panda, chick pea, and rabbit-shaped cakes, pea flour cakes, bean rolls, steamed glutinous rice dumplings

Snacks: Crystal jelly drops, sugar-coated peanuts, fried cashews, fried lobster chips, four candied fruits, pickled peanuts

Vegetables and tofu: Hot cabbage rolls, bamboo shoots with shrimp roe, hot and sour cucumbers, pickled radish, stir-fried mushrooms with celery, bean curd with shrimp

Meats: Salt-boiled pork tenderloin, chicken sticks hot and numbing quail, pot-stew deer soup, stewed bear paw, stir-fried camel hump, fried pheasant with spices, barbequed roast pearl chicken, broiled venison

Rice: Eight Treasures Rice, black rice porridge

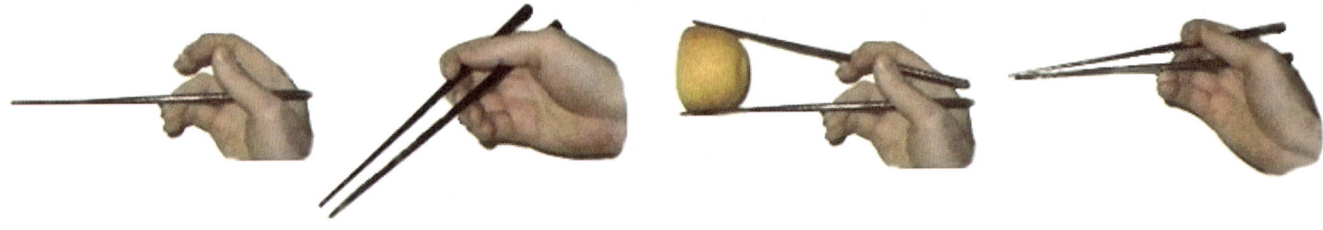

© Copyright 2009 - All rights reserved by OCDF Publications. Single classroom and single event use permitted for purchaser of this book.

Find Your Place at the Banquet Table!

Where each person sits at the table is very important at a formal banquet. Where would you be sitting?

The Grandparents
The grandparents are the most important people at the table. The grandfather will have the seat of honor at the head of the table opposite the door. Remember to greet the grandparents first, as respect is important.

The Guest of Honor
The guests of honor will sit on either side of the grandparents. Female guests of honor are on the left and male guests are on the right.

The Sons and Daughters
If the grandparents have more than one son or daughter, they are seated from oldest to youngest with the oldest son sitting closest to the grandparents. Many families will have the first-born son and his wife sit directly to the right of the grandfather while the second born and his spouse sit directly to the left of the grandmother.

The Other Guests
Guests will be seated between the last of the family members at the foot of the table close to the door.

The Children
The children are placed usually at the foot of the table by the door between the youngest of their parents or their parents' siblings.

Sample Menu for a Chinese Banquet Today:
- Minced seafood in a lettuce wrap
- Honey walnut prawns
- Cantonese barbequed meat platter
- Eight Treasure seafood or shark's fin soup
- Napa cabbage in supreme stock sauce
- Chinese mushrooms with mustard greens
- Chicken stuffed with sticky rice and Chinese sausage
- Stewed duck with dry scallops and black mushrooms
- Braised pork shoulder with angelweed
- Steamed whole fish with ginger and scallion
- Seafood fried rice
- Red bean dessert soup and fresh fruit slices

Everyday Eating
Just like your holiday meals are fancier than your daily dinner, everyday meals in China aren't as elaborate as banquets. There are still some common eating "rules" though. For example, it is rude to use your chopsticks to pick out your favorite foods from a main dish (like all the peanuts from kung pao chicken). It is also considered rude to stab your food with a chopstick. And dropping your chopsticks is bad luck!

Other customs define the correct way to pour tea. Usually, a person will pour tea for other people before pouring a cup for himself or herself. When a cup of tea is poured for you, you are supposed to tap two or three of your fingers on the table. This practice has been followed since the Qīng Dynasty! As the story goes, one emperor was traveling through southern China in disguise. He didn't want to blow his cover, so when he and his attendants stopped at a teahouse, he poured tea for them. When they began to bow, he told them to simply tap the table with their fingers. Two of the fingers represented their bent legs and the third represented their bowed head.

There are some dining manners that are considered rude by Westerners, but are completely fine in China. Rather than waiting until they go home to brush their teeth, people will use toothpicks to clean their teeth right at the table. It is also okay to slurp your soup, lay bones on the tabletop, and make loud noises during a meal. Burps and slurps are considered sounds of enjoyment and gratitude for a meal!

The Origin of Chopsticks
During the time of the great sage kings Yáo 尧 and Shùn 舜, there was a lot of flooding. A man named Yǔ 禹 was put in charge of controlling the waters. During one meal, he put meat into a boiling pot of water. Normally Yǔ and his men would let the meat cool before they could take it out of the pot with their hands. This time, however, Yǔ was impatient and didn't want to waste any time. He chopped two twigs from a tree and used them to pluck the meat from the boiling water. The workers saw that he was able to eat the meat without burning his hands or getting greasy, so one by one, they used twigs too. This is how chopsticks were invented.

Today chopsticks are the main eating utensil in China. Some studies show that when you use chopsticks, you use 80 joints and 50 muscles in your body from your shoulders to your arms, wrist, and fingers.

Student Information Sheet

Student Name _____   Class/Grade Level _____ Date _____

Food as Medicine

When you get sick, you normally take medicine. But when Chinese people get sick, most of them will change what they eat before they take medicine. This is because in ancient times, people didn't have medicines and had to find their own cures. Mixing herbs and plants was tricky and dangerous, so people turned to what they knew best – food!

Using food as medicine is called food therapy or yàoshàn 药膳. In China, it is based on the idea of yīn 阴 and yáng 阳. Yáng represents anything that is bright, dry, or warm, and yīn represents things that are dark, moist, and cool. Chinese believe that both your body and food is either more "yīn" or more "yáng." Your body type changes though because of weather, physical activity, or getting sick. In order to stay healthy, then, you need to balance the yīn and yáng. For example, if you had a fever, you would have a warm, or yáng, body type. To balance your yīn and yáng, you would need to eat "cooling" (yīn) foods like lettuce and cucumber. Eating "heating" (yáng) foods like spicy curry or fried chicken would only make you feel worse.

Knowing your body type and knowing what to eat can be difficult, so people go to Chinese medicine doctors to help them learn what to do. But look at the chart on this page and think about the foods you eat each day. What type of foods do you eat the most?

There is another category of medicinal foods called bǔ 补 foods. Bǔ means "to strengthen" or "to patch up." Bǔ foods, then, are used as a direct cure for what is wrong in your body. These foods might seem strange to you and can also be expensive. In a Chinese medicine shop, you might find foods like deer antler, shark's fin, or bird's nests. Often they are dried out and ground up so you can mix them with hot water or other foods. Another type of bǔ food helps your body parts function better. They can be foods that either look like the body part you are trying to help or are the body part itself. For example, Chinese say that eating walnuts will help your brain because the nut looks like a brain.

Heating
Red, orange, and yellow foods
Most meats, chili pepper, garlic, fried foods, chocolate
Used to treat: low temperature, chills, weakness, diarrhea

Neutral
Pale brown and white foods
Everyday staples like rice or bread

Cooling
Icy white and green foods
Lettuce, cucumber, orange, banana, soy bean
Used to treat: fever, sores, rashes, burns, constipation

The Chinese have different food group and taste categories than what you're used to. The four food groups in China are grains, fruits, meats, and vegetables. Dairy products like milk and cheese are not a regular part of the Chinese diet. A Chinese diet is typically about 40% grains, 30-40% vegetables, 10-15% meats, and the rest is fruits and nuts. The Chinese also have five tastes. You probably know four – sweet, salty, sour, and bitter – but the Chinese add spicy to the list. These five tastes are important in Chinese medicine too. The Chinese believe that each taste is linked to a body part. For example, if you eat a small amount of sweet food, it will help your stomach, but if you eat too much sugar, you can hurt your stomach.

© Copyright 2009 - All rights reserved by OCDF Publications. Single classroom and single event use permitted for purchaser of this book.

Student Information Sheet

Student Name _____   Class/Grade Level _____ Date _____

Food Symbolism

All cultures use objects as symbols to represent an emotion or characteristic. Some symbols are understood in many cultures. For example, when you see a red light, you know it means "Stop!" People in China also understand this simple symbol. Cultures also have symbols that are unique and complicated, so you might not understand them right away. In Chinese culture, there are many, many symbols. Many of them use food!

Fish

For example, the word for a common Chinese fish called carp is lǐ 鲤, which sounds similar to the Chinese word for advantage (lì 利). The fish symbolizes energy, power, and success to Chinese people. Many businesses will put a plastic fish on the wall to bring them good luck. Also, just like a fish jumps out of water, the Chinese believe that they, too, should try to jump over obstacles. When a whole fish is brought to the dinner table, the head should always face the guest or the oldest person. This is to honor them with good luck.

Vegetables

The eggplant, or aubergine, is also symbolic for success. People think that the eggplant looks like a man wearing a hat. Because of this association, sending or receiving this vegetable could mean that a promotion at work is on the way!

Bamboo is one of the most symbolic vegetables in China, though some of its meanings may seem like opposites. For example, because the plant resembles a thin woman, the plant can be associated with youth. But because it is a long-lasting and hardy plant, it is also associated with having a long life.

Noodles

And speaking of age, when it is your birthday, you probably eat cake and ice cream. In China, people eat longevity noodles because they symbolize a long life. These noodles are so long that you need to stand on top of a chair and hold a noodle up in the air in order to see its full length! It is considered unlucky to cut the noodles.

Fruits

Peaches are also given as birthday gifts because they, too, symbolize long life. When peaches are not in season, people will eat buns shaped like peaches.

Oranges and mandarin oranges are another festive gift, usually given during the Spring Festival. They symbolize money due to their golden color.

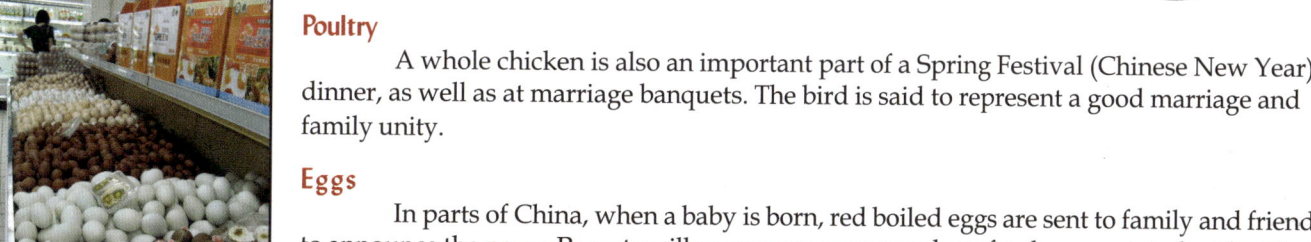

Watermelon (xīguā 西瓜 meaning "western melon") is very popular in the summer. Although in some Chinese dialects, the name sounds similar to the word for death, the fruit is an important symbol for women. On certain Chinese feast days, women will make melon cakes, which they believe will help them bear sons.

Poultry

A whole chicken is also an important part of a Spring Festival (Chinese New Year) dinner, as well as at marriage banquets. The bird is said to represent a good marriage and family unity.

Eggs

In parts of China, when a baby is born, red boiled eggs are sent to family and friends to announce the news. Parents will prepare an even number of red eggs painted with a black dot on one end if the baby is a boy. If the baby is a girl, parents will send an odd number of red eggs without black dots.

© Copyright 2009 - All rights reserved by OCDF Publications. Single classroom and single event use permitted for purchaser of this book.

Traditional Holiday Foods

New Year Celebrations

Chinese people celebrate their most important holiday, called the Spring Festival (chūn jié 春节) or Chinese Lunar New Year, by eating dumplings. On New Year's eve, families sit and chat, make red papercuts, and prepare jiǎozi 饺子, or dumplings. Families will knead the dough and roll it into thin circles, mix and stuff the filling into the circular wraps, and then boil the dumplings. When the clock hits midnight, families eat the dumplings because this symbolizes replacing the old and the changing of the year. People say that jiǎozi look like lumps of silver, so plates of them on the table symbolize making lots of money.

But not every Chinese family celebrates the New Year with the same food. In the southern part of China, people eat glutinous rice balls. People of the Huí 回 minority group in the northwest eat noodles for the first day of the festival. The Zhuàng 壮 minority in the southeast eats large sticky rice cakes that can weigh nearly 2.5 kilograms (6 pounds)! The main food during the Tibetan New Year dinner is gutu, or dough drops. Some gutu are stuffed with stones, wool, hot peppers, charcoal, or coins. These fillings aren't eaten. Instead they are used like fortune tellers to predict a person's future. For example, a stone represents a mean heart, and a coin will bring you good fortune.

Major Festivals

Spring Festival celebrations last about 15 days and finish with the Lantern Festival. Streets and parks are decorated with brightly colored lanterns. People in both northern and southern China eat yuán xiāo 元宵, or glutinous rice balls in soup. In the north, the balls are stuffed with sweet fillings like rose or red bean paste, but in the south, it's common to see sweet, salty, meat, and vegetable yuán xiāo.

About four months later, Chinese celebrate the Dragon Boat Festival to help them remember a famous poet named Qū Yuán 屈原 who worked for the government. Even though he was a good politician, he was sent away. He was so upset that he drowned himself in a river. People from his hometown threw rice into the river to honor him, but they were afraid the fish would eat it. So they wrapped the rice in leaves and tied them with silk thread. Today, the snack zòngzi 粽子 is made by wrapping leaves around sticky rice that has sweet fillings (in the north) or eggs and meat (in the south).

The last major Chinese holiday is the Mid-Autumn Festival held on the 15th day of the eighth lunar month. On this day, there is a full moon, which signifies reunion and happiness. Families will gather to enjoy the moon and eat yuèbǐng 月饼, or moon cakes. Moon cakes are round cookie-like snacks that are supposed to represent the moon. They have been given as gifts to family, friends, and co-workers for over 2,000 years! There are many styles of moon cakes, and the fillings can either be sweet (sugar, lotus paste, or rose petals) or salty (ham, egg, or nuts). The top of the cake is decorated with clouds or the moon. You will see a rabbit on some cakes because the moon goddess has a pet rabbit.

Other Folk Celebrations

In ancient times, when farmers had big harvests, they would hold a làbā 腊八 ceremony. They would invite other people from their village to eat congee, or rice porridge. After Buddhism spread to China, people said the event celebrated the day that the man Sakyamuni (pronounced shock a moo knee) became the Buddha. Sakyamuni had been trying for years to become a Buddha, and he was extremely skinny because he had stopped eating. When he was about to give up, a little girl gave him a bowl of congee. It gave him enough energy to become a Buddha. Today, people still eat congee during the Làbā Festival. They often add red jujubes (zǎo 枣) and chestnuts (lì 栗). Together, these sound like the word zǎolì 早立, which means working hard to have a good harvest.

Another harvest festival is celebrated by the Wǎ 佤 people living in southwestern Yúnnán 云南 Province. Fall is the busiest season to harvest corn. At the start of the New Rice Festival, the Wǎ people pick the corn, ground it into little pieces, boil it, and then serve it with a slice of meat. Each bowl is dedicated to their gods of heaven, earth, mountain, and corn. Then the food is given to the elderly and children.

In many Chinese kitchens, you will see a picture of the Kitchen God. In one legend there is a very, very hungry lord who ate all the delicious food in his palace. When he went looking for more food, he found a woman who had baked sugar cakes. After eating all of them, he asked her to come to the palace and bake them every day. When she said no, he yelled that he would drag her to the palace. She slapped him so hard that he fell against the wall behind the kitchen stove. "Stop being such a pig!" she yelled. "Stay there and watch people eat." Over the years, the lord became known as the Kitchen God, and people hung a picture of him over their stove. Because Chinese people are afraid he will tell the Jade Emperor, or heavenly god, bad things about them, they rub sugar or honey on his picture so he'll tell a "sweetened" version of the story to the Jade Emperor.

Ingredients Required:
1/2 lb. (227 g) Chinese cabbage, finely chopped
1 tsp. (2 g) salt
1 lb. (454 g) ground pork
4 oz. (113 g) Chinese garlic chives, finely chopped
2 1/2 Tbsp. (37 mL) soy sauce
1 Tbsp. (14 mL) rice wine
2 Tbsp. (30 mL) sesame oil
1 Tbsp. (6 g) ginger, finely chopped
2 eggs
Flour for dusting the baking tray
50 dumpling wrappers

Step-by-Step Instructions:
1. To make the filling, combine the cabbage and salt in a bowl and mix together. Let this sit for 30 minutes, then squeeze out all of the water using a towel.
2. Put the cabbage in a large bowl along with the pork, garlic chives, soy sauce, rice wine, sesame oil, ginger, and one egg. Stir until combined and strain out any excess liquid.
3. Put just the egg white from the other egg into a small bowl. Hold the dumpling wrapper on your palm and place a heaping spoonful of filling in the center of the wrapper. Spread a tiny amount of egg white along the edges of the wrapper and fold it into a half-moon shape. Use your thumb and index finger to form small pleats along the sealed edge, pressing the two sides firmly together. Place the dumplings on a baking tray lightly dusted with flour.
4. Bring a large pot of water to boil. Add half of the dumplings, stirring immediately to prevent them from sticking together. Stir gently! Bring the water back to a boil and let the dumplings cook for 8-9 minutes. Alternatively, once it comes back to a boil initially, add a cup of cold water. Then bring it back to a boil and repeat. This is the traditional way to cook dumplings.
5. Remove the dumplings from heat, drain them, and then repeat with the remaining dumplings.

© Copyright 2009 - All rights reserved by OCDF Publications. Single classroom and single event use permitted for purchaser of this book.

Student Information Sheet

Student Name _____   Class/Grade Level _____ Date _____

Inside a Chinese kitchen

There are many, many ways that Chinese food can be prepared. Some methods you might be familiar with because you or someone in your family cooks the same way at home. However, because the Chinese use different kitchen items than you might, there are some ways of preparing food that you won't know. For example, very few Chinese have ovens in their homes or restaurants so they cook food over an open flame. Knowing the words for cooking methods would be very helpful if you were living in China. Some dishes are named by their cooking method, such as kǎo yā 烤鸭 (roast duck).

There are four must-have kitchen utensils in a Chinese kitchen. The most important is a wok. It is made of steel or iron and can have one or two handles. It looks like a wide bowl. It is useful because you can make nearly every single Chinese food in just this one piece of equipment! You will also see metal spatulas with rounded ends. These are larger than Western ones so that you can quickly turn the food. Bamboo steaming baskets are placed over boiling water in the wok. There are also wire straining baskets that can pick up pieces of fried food while allowing the oil to drain off.

The most common methods of cooking in China are stir-frying, steaming, or deep-frying foods. The tools described above are used in these cooking methods. However, there are many, many more ways to cook food. See the extended information handout on the CDRom to learn more!

Stir-fry, chǎo 炒

This is the most common cooking method for Chinese cuisine. It uses a minimal amount of oil that is put into a pre-heated wok. Just before the oil starts smoking, you can add ingredients like garlic, chili peppers, or onions to turn it into fragrant oil. Then you add the main ingredients and stir or toss the foods together. Whatever takes the longest to cook is added first, which is usually meat. If you are also stir-frying vegetables, you remove the meat, cook the vegetables, then return the meat to the wok. You can use a metal spatula to stir the food. A minute before the meat loses its pink color, you add your spice and sauce. Food shouldn't be cooked all the way through while in the wok. This is because it will still cook for a minute or so after it's removed from heat.

Steam, zhēng 蒸

Steaming is done by cooking foods above boiling water. First, you place a wire rack inside the wok, and rest a steaming basket on top of it. Food is then placed in the steaming basket. The steaming time is dependent on the thickness of the food and what texture you'd like the food to be.

Deep fry, zhá 炸

In this method, you fill the wok with several cups of oil. Foods are placed in oil at a relatively high and consistent temperature and fried until they are crisp and golden-brown. It is best to cook small amounts of food and to stir often so that they don't stick together. You can remove the food using a wire strainer. This allows the oil to drain off the food.

© Copyright 2009 - All rights reserved by OCDF Publications. Single classroom and single event use permitted for purchaser of this book.

Student Information Sheet

Student Name _____   Class/Grade Level _____ Date _____

Seasonings and Spices

If you've ever walked down the spice aisle in your grocery store, you've seen just how many flavors you can add to food. Think of a Chinese kitchen like a spice aisle! There are so many flavors to choose from. You probably already know some common ingredients – garlic, chili peppers, and ginger. See how many of the sauces and spices you know from the list below. You can learn about others on the extended information sheet on the CDRom.

Soy Sauce, jiàngyóu 酱油

When it comes to cooking Chinese food, this is the most common ingredient. It can be poured over rice, used in stir-fries, or served as a dipping sauce. Soy sauce was developed about 2,000 years ago and is made by fermenting soy beans with salt and water. Light soy sauce is saltier and used more often in cooking. Dark soy sauce is thicker and used more often as a dipping sauce. Today there are even flavored soy sauces, such as mushroom, fish, or garlic.

Vinegar, cù 醋

This sour "liquid spice" is a very common ingredient in Chinese cooking. Most Chinese vinegars are made by fermenting rice. There are three types: black, red, and white. All of them are weaker than Western vinegars. Black vinegar is sweet and thick. Red vinegar is used most often as a dipping sauce for dumplings, crab, and fried noodles. White vinegar is the most common and can be used in any type of cooking, pickling, sauces, or soups. For example, vinegar combined with salt and a bit of sugar pickles foods. When mixed with soy sauce, spring onions, and ginger, vinegar will reduce the "fishy" taste of seafood. And vinegar in a spicy dish will make it taste less hot.

Sesame Oil, zhīmayóu 芝麻油

Sesame seeds were one of the first plants that were processed into an oil. Unlike the sesame oil produced in some other countries, the Chinese kind is a dark brown color. This is because the seeds are roasted before they are made into oil. This darker sesame oil means that it is not suitable for deep-frying foods, but it is often used in stir-fries or drizzled on top of dishes for added flavor. Some Chinese will make dishes with sesame oil for women who have just had babies because the oil is said to relax and calm the body.

Oyster Sauce, háoyóu 蚝油

Oyster sauce is exactly what it sounds like - a sauce made from oysters - even if it doesn't really taste as "fishy" as you might think. It is a thick, dark liquid that is used to enhance the flavor of stir-fried meats and vegetables. It is especially common in Cantonese cuisine. You'll also see this sauce poured on top of stir-fried vegetables, and it is a main ingredient in a Chinese-American dish you may know quite well - beef with broccoli. Oyster sauce is made by boiling oysters in water. This makes a thick brother that is boiled down until it is even thicker and turns brown. In a real oyster sauce, nothing else would be added. However, today other ingredients are added to the sauce to make it saltier and to make it last longer before it spoils.

Sichuan Peppercorn, huājiāo 花椒

Literally "flower pepper," this famous Sìchuān 四川 spice will leave your mouth numb if you bite into it. They look like berries and grow on bushes. They are usually fried on a dry frying pan. This releases their aroma, which is somewhat citrus-y.

Cumin, zīrán 孜然

This spice is not native to China, but is often used in the cuisine of the northwest. Cumin first came to China from the Middle East along the Silk Road. It is a brownish seed with vertical stripes that has a spicy-sweet aroma and flavor. You'll taste this strong flavor mostly on grilled meats like lamb or chicken kebabs.

Five-spice, wǔxiāngfěn 五香粉

It is believed that the Chinese created this "wonder powder" because they wanted to include the five flavors: salty, sweet, sour, bitter, and spicy. The spice contains cinnamon, star anise or fennel, cumin, cloves, and peppercorns. A favorite Chinese snack is chicken wings rubbed with five-spice.

Star Anise, bājiǎo 八角

This star-like spice has eight points and is the color of rust. It has the smell and taste of licorice, and is usually added to meat dishes. It is a strong spice, so just one star can flavor an entire dish. It is rarely eaten by itself, though a few people will chew the spice as an after-dinner breath freshener.

© Copyright 2009 - All rights reserved by OCDF Publications. Single classroom and single event use permitted for purchaser of this book.

Student Information Sheet

Student Name _____   Class/Grade Level _____ Date _____

Snack Foods

If you were going to reach for a snack, what would you choose? A bag of potato chips? A handful of cookies? An apple or carrot sticks? Chinese children have many of these Western snacks even if they are a bit different. For example, many potato chips have flavors like "fried chicken" or "cucumber shrimp." Even popsicle and ice cream flavors are different. On a hot summer day, you can enjoy a popsicle made with vanilla ice cream and gummy candy or a milk pop that tastes like oatmeal cookies. If you went to an ice cream store, you could purchase flavors like red bean, green pea, or taro root. Sound yummy?

But obviously not all snack foods are Western. All sorts of noodles, dumplings, fried dough, rice rolls, and savory cakes are enjoyed at all times of day. One common favorite throughout China is a stuffed bun. The history of this food begins in the Three Kingdoms Period (220-265 B.C.E.) with a military officer named Zhūgě Liàng 诸葛亮. His army was in southern China when they caught a very severe plague. He created a food, mántóu 馒头 (flour head), which was a dough ball in the shape of a human head and stuffed with meat and vegetables. This was used a sacrifice to the gods, and then he fed it to his soldiers. The southern regions of China have kept the name mántóu for their stuffed buns. But northerners changed the name to bāozi 包子, because bāo means "wrapping."

While some foods are wrapped up like a package, other snacks are eaten on sticks - anything from fruit to starfish. Walk down a street in China, and you'll be able to see vendors selling meat kebabs grilled over hot charcoal or chunks of pineapple cut into a twirly shape. A popular autumn and wintertime treat is the candied hawthorn fruit or bīng táng húlu 冰糖葫芦. This fruit is similar to a crabapple but tarter and is about the size of a ping-pong ball. Just like a candied apple, the fruit is dipped into a boiling sugary mixture that hardens. The tasty snack became popular back during the Sòng 宋 Dynasty (960-1279 C.E.). One of the emperor's concubines was very sick, and none of the imperial doctors knew how to make her better. Then one day, a countryside doctor visited and prescribed a simple remedy: boil haw fruits in sugar water and eat 10 of them a day. The woman was healed! Because sugary haw fruits were a miracle cure, it quickly spread to the common people and became a popular food. Now, these candied skewer snacks also include grapes, kiwi, strawberries, oranges, and walnuts.

Nuts, seeds, and dried fruits are also favorite snacks. Not only do they taste good, but some of these snacks symbolize lucky qualities. For example, peanuts represent a long life and pistachios or kāixīnguó 开心果 sounds like "happy fruit." Melon seeds are dyed red and symbolize joy. They are also said to represent having many children since melons have so many seeds. Sunflower seeds are usually the most popular snack seed because compared to other nuts and seeds, they are the cheapest. Though you usually may eat sunflower seeds that are salted and already taken out of the shell, Chinese people prefer to eat them differently. Because the seeds are still in their shells, people will crack each seed open with their teeth and spit out the shell. The seeds are then eaten one by one. Though it is most common to eat nuts and seeds from April to October, you will always find them as part of the Spring Festival celebrations. It is tradition to visit friends and relatives during this holiday, so families will prepare a tray of nuts, seeds, and candied fruits to present their guests. This platter is called the "Tray of Togetherness" or the "Eight Treasure Tray." The tray is usually in the shape of a circle or an octagon (just like a stop sign) and contains eight snacks.

© Copyright 2009 - All rights reserved by OCDF Publications. Single classroom and single event use permitted for purchaser of this book.

Student Information Sheet

Student Name _____   Class/Grade Level _____ Date _____

Cuisine of Northern China

When you think of China, you probably picture everyone eating rice during their meal. But in northern China, it is more common to see people eating noodles! This is because northern China is very cold and dry, and wheat grows well there. Wheat flour is a very important part of northern Chinese people's diets. They like to eat noodles (miàn 面) and steamed buns (mántou 馒头). If you walk down a street in many northern cities, you will see small stalls that sell meat-stuffed buns (bāozi 包子), dumplings (jiǎozi 饺子), and steaming bowls of noodles. These are popular snacks enjoyed throughout the day!

Northern cuisine can come from any region north of the Yangtze River. If you look at a map of China, you will see just how many regions of China that is! Overall, though, people use a lot of seasonings and spices such as vinegar, garlic, onions, and coriander in their cooking. Most dishes can be made by boiling, steaming, or stir-frying the ingredients. Though these seasonings, spices, and cooking methods are common everywhere, each region adds twists to make their cuisine special.

An important part of northern cuisine comes from Mongolian and Muslim foods. Mongolian hotpot and barbeque are very popular in northern China. To make these dishes, people boil or grill thin slices of meat and vegetables, then stuff the food inside sesame-seed covered buns called shāo bǐng 烧饼. Muslim food is unique because unlike most other Chinese food, it doesn't use any pork. (The religion Islam forbids its followers, Muslims, from eating pork.) In 1760, a Uyghur woman named Xiāng Fēi 香妃 was one of the Qiánlóng 乾隆 Emperor's (1736-1795) many concubines. Because of her Muslim diet, she could only eat certain dishes. Not only were special foods prepared for her at imperial banquets, but the Emperor housed her in a special area of the palace, where he built a Muslim community outside her window so she wouldn't get homesick.

The most well-known type of northern cuisine comes from Běijīng 北京. When emperors ruled China, they would throw very big dinners and entertain a lot of guests. They tried to impress guests with very expensive foods that many people today don't think are very good. It would be hard to find dishes like bear paw, camel hump, and monkey lips on a menu in Běijīng now! The most famous dish today is called Peking Duck, or kǎo yā 烤鸭. It's very crispy duck that you wrap up in thin pancakes like a burrito. Another special food is "squirrel fish," also called Mandarin fish, which is sliced in a criss-cross pattern and then flipped inside out. The fish is fried and then coated in a sweet and sour sauce.

Foods in the northernmost province of Hēilóngjiāng 黑龙江 adopt the ingredients and cooking methods of their surroundings. For example, Hēilóngjiāng is very close to Russia, so you will see a blend of both Chinese and Russian foods in the kitchen. The dishes will be very filling and use a lot of starches like breads, dumplings, and potatoes. In Inner Mongolia, you taste the influence of Mongolian, Chinese, and Muslim cultures in the cooking, so food there has a lot of lamb, onions, and garlic.

What do people eat?

Breakfast: Bāozi 包子 - a bun filled with minced pork and onions or yóutiáo 油条 - fried dough or zhōu 粥 - congee or jiānbǐng 煎饼 - an egg pancake with sauce or mántou 馒头 - a steamed bun

Lunch: Zhájiàngmiàn 炸酱面 – noodles with fermented bean paste and meat sauce or stir-fried dishes of vegetables and meat or yángròu chuànr 羊肉串 – BBQ lamb kebabs

Dinner: Běijīng kǎo yā 北京烤鸭 (Peking Duck as the last course of a special dinner). A home-style or a typical restaurant dinner would include cold dishes, vegetable dishes, meat dishes, and fruit for dessert. Dishes commonly have cabbage or onions with pork, beef, or mutton. Family meals often include noodles or dumplings.

© Copyright 2009 - All rights reserved by OCDF Publications. Single classroom and single event use permitted for purchaser of this book.

Student Information Sheet

Student Name _____   Class/Grade Level _____ Date _____

Cuisine of Eastern China

Because eastern China is part of the Lower Yangtze River Valley and touches the Pacific Ocean, the food in this region is what the Chinese call "land meets water." Not only are there the regular meats like chicken, but people will often cook with crab, shrimp, and water plants like seaweed. Because there is so much seafood, there is vinegar in many dishes. Vinegar kills the taste of bad water and also washes away any salt left on the seafood from the ocean. Another special trait of the food of eastern China is that simple foods like cabbage are made very special by slightly changing the quantity and quality of oils, vinegars, and cooking wines.

Eastern China is home to four of the Eight Great Traditions, or eight great cuisines: !nhuī 安徽, Fújiàn 福建, Shāndōng 山东, and Zhèjiāng 浙江. Fújiàn and Shāndōng specialize in seafood and soups. In Fújiàn alone, 167 types of fish and 90 kinds of shellfish and turtles are served! One of the most well-known dishes is a soup called Buddha Jumps over the Wall. Seafood, chicken, duck, and pork are put in a rice wine jar and cooked for hours over a fire. Though many Buddhists don't eat meat, this soup is thought to smell so good that even Buddha would jump over a wall to eat it.

One of Zhèjiāng's famous dishes is called Beggar's Chicken. According to the legend, a hungry, homeless man found a chicken. Because he didn't have a stove to cook it, he covered the chicken in mud and leaves and baked it over a fire. Then, the emperor walked by and wanted to know what smelled so delicious. The dish was named "Beggar's Chicken" and added to the menu at the emperor's palace. Some people today don't care for the name of this dish, so on menus you might also see it listed as Noble Chicken.

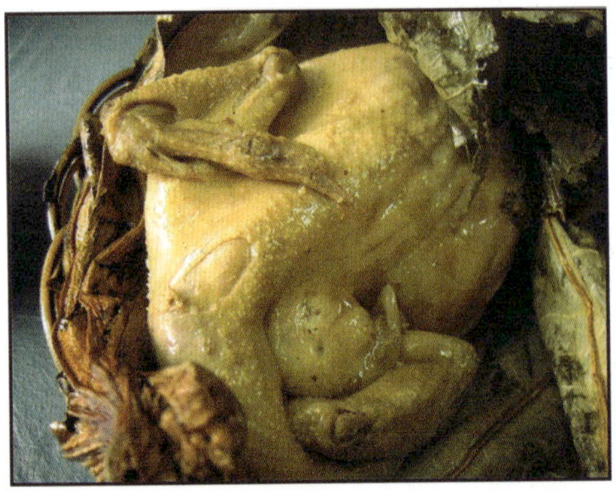

What do people eat?

Breakfast: Congee with dried seafood **or** preserved green plums **or** tea eggs **or** flavored rice wrapped in a lotus leaf

Lunch: Soup with noodles or dumplings called wontons abroad but called hún dun 馄饨 in Shànghǎi 上海 **or** soup with mini-fish from Tàizhōu 泰州 Lake **or** sweet lotus root

Dinner: Marinated five-spice spare ribs **or** fish with ginkgo nuts **or** preserved bean curd and vegetables **or** textured jellyfish **or** fried sardines **or** hairy crab **or** Beggar's Chicken **or** steamed fish

!nhuī is not on the coast like other eastern provinces, but is near Huáng Shān 黄山 (Yellow Mountain). Many of !nhuī's foods such as stone frog, wild mushrooms, bay berries, tea leaves, and bamboo come from the mountain. One of !nhuī's famous dishes is called Lǐ Hóngzhāng 李鸿章 hotchpotch. A hotchpotch is a thick soup with many ingredients. Lǐ Hóngzhāng was a top official in the Qīng 清 Dynasty (1616-1911). During a visit to the United States, he hosted a banquet. When there wasn't much food left, he asked the cooks to combine all of the remaining ingredients into a stew. The delicious dish of sea cucumber, squid, tofu, ham, mushrooms, and chicken is still served today.

The most well-known city in eastern China is Shànghǎi 上海 and its food is influenced by the cuisines from the surrounding provinces. Like other coastal regions, Shanghai offers many seafood dishes, and is best known for the hairy crab. The hairy crab, or dà zhá xiè 大闸蟹, is found in the Yangtze River, and is generally tied up in strings, steamed in a bamboo basket and eaten. Yet what the city is most famous for is its small soup dumplings called xiǎo lóng bāo 小笼包. Some people will pop the entire bun into their mouth so that the soup doesn't squirt out when they bite it! However, it is also common to nibble off the twisted top of the dumpling, suck out all the soup, then dip it in vinegar before eating it.

© Copyright 2009 - All rights reserved by OCDF Publications. Single classroom and single event use permitted for purchaser of this book.

Student Information Sheet

Student Name _____   Class/Grade Level _____ Date _____

Cuisine of Western China

Today western China is considered the "spicy zone." When you eat dishes from the provinces of Sìchuān 四川 (you might have also seen Szechuan) or Húnán 湖南, for example, your tongue will feel very hot and numb at the same time. This is because of the spices in the food. But food in this region of China wasn't always spicy. Several thousand years ago, people who lived there really liked sweet food!

The two most common spices are the chili pepper and the Sìchuān peppercorn. The chili arrived from South America in the 17th century. It is red and very spicy, and it "burns" your tongue. The peppercorn looks like a small, black flower and smells a little bit like citrus fruit. When you bite into it, your tongue goes numb. Spicy foods are popular in western China because it is very humid there. Humidity makes it hard for the body to get rid of extra water, but spicy food makes you sweat!

What do people eat?

Breakfast: Rice flour pancakes stuffed with banana and lotus paste

Lunch: Yú xiāng ròu sī 鱼香肉丝 – "fish fragrance" shredded pork or má pó dòufu 麻婆豆腐-tofu with ground pork and chili sauce or dàndàn miàn 担担面-pork and chili sauce over noodles

Dinner: Pickled vegetables over rice or tea-smoked duck or shuǐ zhǔ yú 水煮鱼-fish boiled in chili oil or twice-cooked pork or gōng bǎo jī dīng 宫爆鸡丁-kung pao chicken or là jī dīng 辣鸡丁 - chicken and large red chilis or yú xiāng qié zi 鱼香茄子-braised eggplant with chili sauce

The food of western China also has a lot of garlic in it. Garlic is combined with chili peppers in one sauce called yú xiāng 鱼香. This means "fish fragrance," but there is nothing fishy about it! There are several important rivers flowing though Sìchuān, so it got its name which means "four rivers." However, Sìchuān is quite far from the sea and is surrounded by mountains. One legend says that there was a Sichuanese cook who created yú xiāng based on the fish he had never tasted but had always heard about it. The sauce is very popular now all around China and is usually eaten on shredded pork or eggplant cubes.

You probably know the dish kung pao chicken, or gōng bǎo jī dīng 宫爆鸡丁. There are many stories about how this dish was named. Some say that it was named for the general whose son accidentally dropped a handful of chili peppers into a wok of fried chicken. Another says that this dish was named after an army official who lived in a castle because it was his favorite dish. It doesn't really matter which story is true, but it shows that naming food after an important person gives a dish a better status.

Though Sìchuān is the most well-known type of food from western China, the food from other regions is very tasty too. For example, food from Máo Zédōng's 毛泽东 home province, Húnán, is also very spicy. When he was in Běijīng 北京 setting up the People's Republic of China, he had chefs from his hometown visit just to make him his favorite foods. Though similar to Sìchuān and Húnán cuisines, food from the Guìzhōu 贵州 region mixes the tastes of sour and spicy. The area is also known for its unique salt-pickled vegetables. Cuisine from Yúnnán 云南 is also usually spicy and sour. The people there often use dairy products because of how close they are to India and Tibet. These areas do use dairy products like milk and yogurt in their cooking. This is unique because many Chinese don't eat dairy products because foods with milk make them sick.

© Copyright 2009 - All rights reserved by OCDF Publications. Single classroom and single event use permitted for purchaser of this book.

Student Information Sheet

Student Name _____   Class/Grade Level _____ Date _____

Cuisine of Southern China

What do people eat?
Breakfast: Fried dough sticks dipped in soy milk or zhōu 粥 congee – rice porridge
Lunch: Dim sum: boiled bok choy with oyster sauce, barbeque pork-filled buns, minced shrimp and pork dumplings, roasted duck and glass noodle soup, glutinous rice wrapped in mango and rolled in coconut
Dinner: Shark fin soup or shrimp and bean pods in a taro nest or pigeon and tofu in brown sauce, or warm bean sprouts or noodles and pork strips stir-fried on an iron skillet and red bean pastry for desert

Northern Chinese people say that the southern Chinese will "eat anything that swims except submarines, anything that flies except airplanes, and anything that has legs except tables." Does that sound silly to you? People say this because even though southern dishes contain foods like chicken, pork, and beef, they also cook with snakes, insects, dog, birds' nests, animal stomachs, and chicken feet. Even if you think some of those foods sound "weird" or "gross," many Chinese people think that southern food (also called Cantonese food or yuè cài 粤菜) is some of the best in China. Cantonese food is considered to be one of the Eight Great Cuisines of China.

Cantonese food is also the most popular outside of China. When you order from a Chinese restaurant at home, you are probably eating some kind of southern food. This is because most Chinese immigrants come from southern China. They try to bring the foods they like with them. Cantonese food is also the best-tasting to many Westerners because it is not too spicy and doesn't use many new or strange spices. You probably know foods like fried rice, chop suey, and chow mein. Though these dishes are delicious, they aren't "special" dishes because they are made with leftover meat and vegetables and old rice or noodles. Southern Chinese like to eat very, very fresh foods. They like to eat vegetables harvested the same day they're bought. They also eat a lot of fish and seafood. When you go to a grocery store, you normally see cut-up pieces of fish lying in ice. But in southern China, you would see fishermen bringing their fish right into a store or restaurant so people can choose their own live seafood. Southern Chinese like to taste the natural flavors of their foods, too, so they don't add many spices or sauces to their dishes.

One southern Chinese region, the special administrative region of Macau, however, is special because of its use of spices. The food here is a blend of southern Chinese and Portuguese cuisine. The many ingredients and spices include those from Europe, Africa, and southeast Asia. Also unlike many Chinese cuisines, the most common cooking methods are baking, grilling, and roasting. Some of the more famous Macanese dishes are bacalhau, a salty dried cod, and egg custard tarts.

Dim sum is a very popular snack food in southern China, especially in Hong Kong and Guǎngdōng 广东. Think of them as little appetizers or tapas. Many dim sum dishes are types of dumplings stuffed with seafood, meat, vegetables, or sweet pastes. Dim sum is eaten as a mid-morning snack or for lunch. In a Hong Kong dim sum restaurant, waitresses will push metal carts stacked with round bamboo baskets around the dining room. When they come to your table, you open each lid until you find a dim sum dish that you want to eat. It's like a personal buffet!

The most important part of any southern Chinese meal is a bowl of rice. Some people will say they haven't eaten at all if they do not eat rice with their meal. The average southern Chinese person will eat 136 kilograms (300 pounds) of rice a year! That's about the same weight as an adult panda! Can you imagine how much rice that would be? They eat so much rice because it grows well in southern China. Rice needs a lot of water to grow, and southern China is very warm and rainy. Rice farmers can sometimes grow up to three crops a year.

© Copyright 2009 - All rights reserved by OCDF Publications. Single classroom and single event use permitted for purchaser of this book.

Student Information Sheet

Student Name _____   Class/Grade Level _____ Date _____

Cuisine of the Minority Groups

If someone asked you to describe the food in your country in just one or two dishes, what would you say? Is all American food hamburgers and hot dogs or is all British food scones and fish'n'chips? You would say that there are many kinds of food in your country based on ethnic groups that were either originally in the country (native groups) or people who moved there (migrants). It is the same in China. Even though regions of China may have similar ingredients or cooking methods, the foods can be very different. There are 55 different ethnic minority groups living in China. Each group has different customs and languages, so imagine how many different foods they make to eat! Some people are native to the region they inhabit, and some people came to China as migrants across trade routes and brought their foods with them.

The most common meat in China is pork, but you won't often see it in Tibet (southwest China). Tibet is so high above sea level that it is hard to raise pigs, cows, fruits, and vegetables. Tibetans mostly eat a grain called barley. They ground it into a flour then mix it with yak butter. This makes a doughy paste called tsamba that Tibetans eat with their hands.

You won't see pork on a menu in a Muslim Chinese restaurant, either. Muslims do not eat pork because of their religious beliefs. This ethnic group lives primarily in Gānsù 甘肃 Province and Níngxià Huí 宁夏回 and Xīnjiāng 新疆 Uyghur autonomous regions. These are people who migrated to China from the Middle East. Their dishes are often made with beef or lamb and have lots of onions, garlic, and cumin. You will often see chuàn 串 (meat kebabs), lā miàn 拉面 (spicy broth soup with beef and noodles), lā tiáo zi 拉条子 (Xīnjiāng noodles with lam-band potatoes), and niú ròu bǐng 牛肉饼 (crispy buns filled with beef). Because of the Turkish influence on Xīnjiāng food, you will also see a variety of breads that are stuffed with meats and dipped in a cheese-like yogurt when eaten.

There is one story about a Muslim man who owned a small restaurant in Gānsù Province. Even though his lamb dishes were delicious, he never had any customers. He wanted to rent a restaurant in a busier part of town but didn't have enough money. So he put his lamb into wooden buckets and carried them through the streets. The dish, "spicy lamb in a bucket," is still a popular street food in Gānsù today!

Some ethnic minorities don't eat meat at all, like the Turkish and Mongol nomads. These people are constantly moving around northern China. The animals are more valuable for carrying things than for eating, so the nomads eat a lot of bread, porridge, yogurt, and a drink called kumys (fermented horse's milk). Another group of people who don't eat meat is Buddhist monks and nuns. Although the Buddha was not a vegetarian, some Buddhist groups won't eat meat because they consider it violent towards animals. Most Chinese Buddhist monks and nuns will not eat meat, but Tibetan monks and nuns do not follow this rule.

Other people, like members of the Dǎi 傣 Nationality who live in Yúnnán 云南 Province, eat insects. They also eat a lot of meat, rice, and bitter-tasting vegetables, but insects are also a common part of their diet. Because the weather in their area is hot and humid, there are a lot of bugs. The Dǎi people eat a lot of dishes and snacks made of insects. They eat cicadas, bamboo worms, spiders, and ant eggs. The Wǎ 瓦, or Va, people who also live in Yúnnán often eat several kinds of caterpillars. They will mix the insects into rice porridge with vegetables, salt, and chili pepper. Another smaller Yúnnán group called the Drung (Dúlóng 独龙) eat bee

People of the Zhuàng 壮 minority who live mostly in Guǎngxī Zhuàng 广西壮 Autonomous Region eat foods you may consider strange. In addition to crispy bees and spiced insects, Zhuàng people enjoy eating dog, animal liver, and even pig's blood. Would you like to try any of these foods?

© Copyright 2009 - All rights reserved by OCDF Publications. Single classroom and single event use permitted for purchaser of this book.

pupae. A pupa is the stage of an insect between larvae and adult that lives in a cocoon. There are several members of the Drung minority who are over the age of 100. They say it is because they eat bee pupae regularly that they can live so long.

The Miáo 苗, people, who live mostly in Guìzhōu 贵州 Province and Guǎngxī but can also be found in Húnán 湖南 Province, pay a lot of attention to dinner etiquette. When they have a visitor, they kill a chicken. The oldest guest receives the chicken head and the youngest guest receives the chicken leg. Another custom is sharing the chicken heart. The oldest dinner guest will pick up the heart with his or her chopsticks and offer it to the visitor. However, the visitor shouldn't eat the whole chicken heart, but instead, share it with the oldest family members. Can you think of any food customs like this? What about snapping a wish bone?

Some ethnic minority groups are well-known for their cooking methods. For example, the Pǔmǐ 普米 nationality from Yúnnán is known for their cakes and cookies, but they aren't the same type you are used to. These are made from a mixture of oatmeal, water, salt, and oil. Adults will eat hard-cooked cakes, but the elderly and children are served soft-baked cookies. Flattened dough balls are brushed with oil, and then stuck onto clean tree branches. Then they are baked over a fire, which make them very crispy. The Nàxī 纳西 people also are known for their cakes called baba. The flour cakes can be stewed in a covered pot until they're golden, roasted on a stone until puffy, or put on the edge of a pot that is cooking potatoes and melons.

Another minority group who lives in Yúnnán, the Blang (Bùlǎng 布朗), are known for their bamboo tube rice. Instead of simply boiling or steaming the rice, they cover rice with pulp from the bamboo plant. This gives it a nice flavor. It's then stuffed into a hollow bamboo tube and roasted over a charcoal fire. Though they will eat raw meat, they also enjoy eating preserved meat. They do this by packing cooked meat with lots of salt. This allows the meat to stay fresh for a long time.

Other groups are known for their drinks, such as the Lìsù 傈僳. These people live along a river in Yúnnán and make wines from fruits and grains. They make a fruit vinegar with peaches and pears in the summertime. They also make a yellow wine out of barley, corn, wheat, and mountain spring water. They mix it all in a clay pot and let it ferment. Several days later, they'll drink the strong-smelling liquid. The Bái 白 people of Yúnnán drink tea twice a day. They have their first cup of "morning tea" right after they wake up. They drink another cup at noon called "thirst-satisfying tea." The tea is often served with milk and even popcorn.

Student Information Sheet

Student Name _____   Class/Grade Level _____ Date _____

The Culture of Tea

One of the world's most famous drinks, tea, was discovered by accident! Shén Nóng 神农, the Chinese god of farming, was boiling water to drink when he noticed a few leaves had blown into the cup. He tasted the brownish water and thought it was delicious. Since then, about 5,000 years ago, tea has been the most popular drink in China.

There are six types of tea in China, but you're probably most familiar with black and green teas. Black tea comes from the southern region of Fújiàn 福建 Province and is the most widely drunk tea outside of China and Japan. Ninety percent of the black tea harvested in China is sent to other countries! Black tea comes from green tea plants, but it is exposed to chemicals that turn it dark and give it a stronger taste. Green tea is just steamed and dried.

One of the most famous green teas is Lóngjǐng 龙井 tea. It comes from Hángzhōu 杭州, which is one of China's most beautiful citites. Lóngjǐng tea is clear and tastes sweet and fresh. It takes a lot of skill to harvest this tea correctly. The people who pick the leaves say that if you pick the leaves three days early, the tea is a treasure. But if you pick the leaves three days late, the tea is trash.

There is a famous story about the Qiánlóng 乾隆 Emperor and Lóngjǐng tea. When he was traveling in southern China, he was amazed at the skill of the tea pickers and wanted to learn himself. But when he started, he was told that his mother was very sick and that he had to go home to Běijīng 北京. When his mother saw him, she only felt half better. She smelled something sweet on him, and when he realized there were a few tea leaves stuck in his sleeve, he put them into water and made tea. The queen was instantly cured! The Emperor ordered that Lóngjǐng tea be called "Royal Tea," and it made the green tea even more famous.

Chinese people also enjoy tea made from flowers. Chrysanthemum tea is made by soaking dried flowers in hot water. It makes a light yellowish-brown tea that you drink with a lump of rock sugar. It can help you get over flu symptoms, a sore throat, and a fever. Jasmine tea is also a favorite but it is made differently. The jasmine flower only blooms at night. It is picked and mixed with green tea leaves for several days. It takes about four or five days for the tea leaves to absorb the flavor and smell of the jasmine. Then the jasmine has no more scent, so they are removed. The jasmine-scented tea leaves are then mixed with boiling water to make jasmine tea.

The reasons for drinking tea have changed throughout Chinese history. For some, tea has been a medicine. At other times, tea inspired imperial competitions. Today you will see people carrying thermoses filled with tea, or you might see businessmen making business deals in a teahouse. In southern China, especially, you will see formal tea ceremonies called gōngfu chá 工夫茶. In today's Chinese tea ceremony, a teapot about the size of a fist and cups the size of tennis balls split in half are used. The tea cups are so small because the tea is supposed to be drunk in one sip. The pot and cups are rinsed in boiling water. The cups are then placed together and the tea is poured quickly in a circle from one cup to another without stopping. The first round of tea is thrown out (it is only meant to rinse the leaves) and the second round is drunk. People first observe the color, smell the tea next, and then they drink it.

© Copyright 2009- All rights reserved by OCDF Publications. Single classroom and single event use permitted for purchaser of this book.

Student Information Sheet

Student Name _____   Class/Grade Level _____ Date _____

Agriculture

China is home to about 1.3 billion people, which is about one fifth of the world's population. Finding a way to feed that many people has been a big challenge. This is why agriculture is so important in China. Agriculture includes maintaining land, growing crops, and raising animals. But only about 14% of China's land is arable, or suitable for growing crops! That makes growing vegetables or raising cows and chickens more difficult. However, because China is so big, it has many different types of terrain (surface of the land) and climates (weather). Because of this, Chinese people can grow different types of food all over the country. Rice, for example, grows better in warm, moist climates and on terraced land that looks like steps. An important ingredient in bread and noodles, wheat, grows best in cold, dry climates, so it is a common crop in northern China. Look at the map of China below to discover what grows and is raised where!

© Copyright 2009 - All rights reserved by OCDF Publications. Single classroom and single event use permitted for purchaser of this book.

Student Information Sheet

Student Name _____   Class/Grade Level _____ Date _____

Imports and Exports

One of the best ways to experience a different culture is through its food. Sometimes, you don't even have to leave your own town to do this! In big cities around the world today, you can taste foods from all over. You could eat a French crepe for breakfast, a meat and vegetable kebab from the Middle East for lunch, and then an African meat and rice dish that you eat with your hands for dinner. The reason you can sample all of these foods is because of the business of import and export, or trade, between countries. It is also due to the migration of people throughout the world. That's likely how Chinese food came to your country!

An import is something that you bring "in" from somewhere else, usually another country. An export is the opposite. An export is something that you send "out" to somewhere else in the world. You can export anything from food, to clothing, or even ideas! Many times importing and exporting is done for business purposes. For example, Chinese people learned how to weave beautiful silks – a product that people in Central Asia and Europe didn't have. Over hundreds of years, merchants formed a series of trade routes called the Silk Road. Chinese traders exchanged silk for other valuable products from different countries and cultures. The Chinese exported silk and imported Buddhism, Western instruments, and scientific technology.

Food was also exchanged along the Silk Road. Noodles were invented in China around 300 B.C.E. This staple food was then passed to the West, specifically Italy, today's famous pasta home. But the West also influenced noodle-making in China. When the Roman Empire entered the Silk Road trade, they brought the grindstone with them. With this tool, Chinese were able to grind wheat into flour. Instead of using it to make breads like in Europe or the Middle East, they continued to make different noodles like the dumpling. China also sent tea to Europe which became an instant favorite. Spices from Central Asia were sent to China, which changed the flavors of Chinese dishes, especially in the northwest. In places like Xīnjiāng 新疆, food is very similar to what you'd eat in the Middle East with flat breads, lamb kebabs, and spices like cumin.

Imports and exports have only grown for China today. China is one of the world's biggest exporters today! One of the biggest exports is black tea. Most Chinese people prefer green tea, so 90% of the black tea grown in China is sent to other countries. China also continues to be a top exporter of rice, along with several other Southeast Asian countries. Also, in 2006, China exported 12% of the world's total fruit and vegetables. Next time you are in the grocery store, see how many Chinese snacks, spices, and sauces you can find. Do you see oyster sauce, chili paste, soy sauce, rice crackers, or shrimp chips? China is a surplus country. This means that China produces a majority of its own food. China's biggest imports are generally machinery and brand-name luxury items and technology.

A challenge for importing and exporting today is food safety. Countries have different standards for how food needs to be treated – from the fertilizers used to grow it, to the temperature of the refrigerator boxes used to transport it to other countries. Another concern is about a business term called "free trade." Some countries establish relationships that allow them to import and export products without government restriction. However, other countries make traders pay lots of tax money to bring products into the country. Governments and organizations are constantly working to make it safer and easier to import and export foods around the world.

© Copyright 2009 - All rights reserved by OCDF Publications. Single classroom and single event use permitted for purchaser of this book.

Student Recipe - Cuisine of Northern China

Fried Meat and Bean Sauce Noodles
Zhá jiàng miàn 炸酱面 (pronounced: jah jee-ahng me-an)

Introduction:
Zhá jiàng miàn 炸酱面 is a traditional northern Chinese noodle dish, but it has become popular in other parts of the country. In Běijīng 北京, cooks will use yellow soybean paste, but in other parts of China, you'll see chefs use sweet noodle sauce (tián miàn jiàng 甜面酱) or hoisin sauce (hǎi xiān jiàng 海鲜酱, which is the same sauce used in Peking Duck. This has also become a popular dish in Korea. They make it with a roasted soybean sauce and will add shrimp instead of pork.

Ingredients Required:
2 cups (200 g) soybean paste
2 cups (200 g) water
1/4 lb. (100 g) ground pork (use tofu instead for a vegetarian version)
1 lb. (500 g) pre-cooked noodles
1 Tbsp. (6 g) garlic, minced
1 Tbsp. (6 g) green onion, minced
1 Tbsp. (6 g) ginger, minced
Cucumber, sliced in julienne style
Cutting board
Knife (please get help from a parent/teacher)
Pot
Wok

Step-by-Step Instructions:
Students should gain the assistance and supervision of a parent/teacher for this activity.
1. Put noodles into a pot of boiling water and cook until tender. Drain and set aside.
2. Prepare ingredients. Mince garlic, green onion, and ginger. Set aside. Julienne (cut into match sticks) the cucumbers. Set aside. Mix the soybean paste with water in a bowl. Set aside. Break the ground meat into pieces.
3. Heat the wok and add oil. When oil is hot, add the pork and stir-fry until it is golden brown.
4. Add the garlic, green onion, and ginger to the meat and stir-fry until golden brown.
5. Add the soy bean paste and simmer the mixture for 10 minutes, stirring frequently.
6. Pour the sauce over the pre-cooked noodles.
7. Garnish the dish with the cucumbers.

3.   4.   5.   6.

Contributed by: Chef Lǐ Gāoyáng 李高杨, Tiān Wài Tiān 天外天 Restaurant in Běijīng 北京, China

© Copyright 2009 - All rights reserved by OCDF Publications. Single classroom and single event use permitted for purchaser of this book.

Student Recipe - *Cuisine of Eastern China*

Steamed Fish

Qīng zhēng yú 清蒸鱼 (pronounced: ching jung you)

Ingredients Required: 
1 whole fish, tilapia, bass, or carp (preferred)
3 Tbsp. (20 g) green onion, shredded
3 Tbsp. (20 g) ginger, shredded
4 Tbsp. (60 mL) fish sauce
Knife (please get help from a parent/teacher)
Cutting board
Wok
Steam rack

Step-by-Step Instructions:
Students should gain the assistance of a parent/teacher for this activity.
1. Purchase a whole fish from the market. Have it scaled, but keep the skin and bones.
2. At home, rinse the fish thoroughly.
3. Use a sharp knife to make two long cuts on either side of the top middle ridge of the fish. Also slit the bottom of the fish in half and make two perpendicular cuts at the top and bottom of this cut. Arrange fish on a plate. Slightly pull the flesh away from the bone as shown in the picture.
4. Top the fish with green onion and ginger.
5. Pour sauce in the dish around the fish.
6. Place the steaming rack in the wok and pour some water into the wok. Place the fish plate on top of the rack.
7. When the water boils, cover the fish and steam for 15 minutes.

Contributed by: Tiānwàitiān 天外天 Restaurant in Běijīng 北京, China

© Copyright 2009 - All rights reserved by OCDF Publications. Single classroom and single event use permitted for purchaser of this book.

Student Recipe- *Cuisine of Western China*

Kung Pao Chicken with Peanuts
Gōng bào jī dīng 宫爆鸡丁 (pronounced: gong bao gee ding)

Introduction:
There are many stories about how this dish, gōng bào jī dīng 宫保鸡丁, got its name. In fact, many of them are included in various places throughout this book! One of the most popular is that an official had a mischievous son. One day, while the chef was preparing dinner in the kitchen, the young boy accidentally dropped a handful of chili peppers into a wok full of stir-fried chicken. The dish was so tasty that it became a favorite and spread from Sìchuān 四川 to all over the world!

Ingredients Required:
1/2 lb.(250 g) boneless, skinless chicken breast
  (you can substitute shrimp or eggplant in this recipe)
7 oz. (200 g) deep-fried peanuts
3 Tbsp. (44 mL) soy sauce
2 Tbsp. (30 mL) rice wine
2 Tbsp. (30 mL) sesame oil
1 tsp. (2 g) Sichuan peppercorn
2 Tbsp. (30 mL) Sichuan chili sauce
1 Tbsp. (6 g) ginger, chopped
1 Tbsp. (6 g) green onion, chopped
1 tsp. (2 g) salt
3 tsp. (6 g)sugar
Cooking oil
Knife (please get help from a parent/teacher)
Cutting board
Wok

Step-by-Step Instructions:
Students should gain the assistance and supervision of a parent/teacher for this activity.
1. Cut the chicken into small cubes. Set aside. Chop the green onion into similar-sized segments. Roughly chop the ginger. Set the other ingredients aside as well.
2. Heat the wok and add cooking oil. When hot, add the chicken and stir-fry until slightly golden. Add the peanuts and green onion to the wok and continue to stir-fry.
3. Remove ingredients from wok and drain.
4. Reheat wok and add a bit of cooking oil. When hot, add ginger and Sichuan chili sauce and briefly stir-fry.
5. Add the soy sauce, rice wine, sesame oil, and Sichuan peppercorn to the wok. After cooking a bit, add the chicken, onions, and peanuts back to the wok. Stir to coat.
6. Place the food onto the plate and serve immediately.

3.

4.
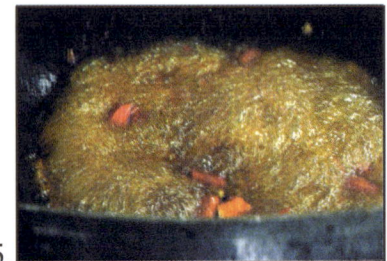
5.

Contributed by: Chef Fàn Yíntāo 范银涛, Tiān Wài Tiān 天外天 Restaurant in Běijīng 北京, China

Student Recipe - Cuisine of Southern China

Sweet and Sour Pork
Táng cù lǐ jī 糖醋里脊 (pronounced: tong tsu lee gee)

Introduction:
For each of the 12 years on the Chinese Lunar Year calendar, there is a corresponding animal. In 2007, China released a set of postage stamps with a cute cartoon picture of pig and her piglets. But that wasn't enough. It was a scratch-and-sniff stamp that smelled – and tasted! – like sweet and sour pork. Though other countries had made scratch-and-sniff stamps (Hong Kong – tea, Switzerland – chocolate, for example), this was the first time that a stamp smelled like a popular dish. You don't have to go in search of these unique stamps to get a taste of the famous Chinese dish, however. Try out this recipe for an authentic version of the pork dish you get in Chinatown.

Ingredients Required:
1/2 lb. (250 g) battered pork loin, cut into bite-sized pieces
  (you can substitute chicken or shrimp in this recipe)
1/2 red pepper, chopped
1/2 green pepper, chopped
Sweet and sour sauce
Cooking oil
2 small bowls
Knife (please get help from a parent/teacher)
Cutting board
Wok

Batter:
1/3 cup (33 g) flour
1/3 cup (33 g) cornstarch
1 egg white, lightly beaten
1 Tbsp. (15 mL) oil
Water, as needed

Sweet and Sour Sauce:
1 Tbsp. (6 g) cornstarch
4 Tbsp. (60 mL) water
2 Tbsp. (30 mL) ketchup
2 Tbsp. (30 mL) rice vinegar
2 Tbsp. (30 mL) soy sauce
1/4 cup (25 g) sugar

Step-by-Step Instructions:
Students should gain the assistance and supervision of a parent/teacher for this activity.

1. In a small bowl, make the batter for your pork. Combine the flour and corn. Separate the yolk from the egg white and pour the egg white into the dry mixture. Stir in the egg white and the oil. Add water as needed to make the batter thin enough to drop off the spoon but not so thin that it is runny. Set aside.
2. In another small bowl, prepare your sweet and sour sauce. Dissolve the cornstarch in the water. When mixed, add the rest of the sauce ingredients. Stir to mix. Set aside.
3. Chop the peppers and pork into bite-size pieces.
4. Dip the pork into the batter. Each piece should be well-coated.
5. Heat the wok and fill ¼ full of oil. When hot, deep-fry the pork in small batches until golden brown and crispy. Remove and drain the pork. Repeat this process until all of the pork is fried.
6. Reheat the wok and pour in the sweet and sour sauce. Bring to a boil and allow sauce to thicken.
7. As the sauce is just about thick, add in the peppers and cook until almost tender.
8. Add in the pork and toss to coat the meat and vegetables. Place the food onto a plate and serve immediately.

4a.

4b.

5.

Contributed by: Chef Fàn Yíntāo 范银涛, Tiān Wài Tiān 天外天 Restaurant in Běijīng 北京, China

© Copyright 2009 - All rights reserved by OCDF Publications. Single classroom and single event use permitted for purchaser of this book.

References and Resources

Create a China's Foods library!

Chinese Food

A Cook's Guide to Chinese Vegetables by Martha Dahlen. ISBN: 9627502545.
A Food-lover's Journey Around China published by Foreign Languages Press. ISBN-13: 9787119041759.
Origins of Chinese Cuisine published by Asiapac. ISBN: 9812293175.
Origins of Chinese Food Culture published by Asiapac. ISBN: 9812293183.
Origins of Chinese Tea and Wine published by Asiapac Comics. ISBN: 9812293698.
All the Tea in China by Kit Chow and Ione Kramer. ISBN: 0835121941.
Chinese Foods by Liu Junru. ISBN: 7508506138.
Chinese Food Finder: Guide to Regional Chinese Cuisines by Carl Chu. ISBN: 1932296093.
China to Chinatown: Chinese Food in the West by J.A.G. Roberts. ISBN: 1861891334.

Stories about Chinese Food

Food and Chinese Culture: Essays on Popular Cuisines by Zishan Chen. ISBN: 159265049X.
Moonbeams, Dumplings, & Dragon Boats: A Treasury of Chinese Holiday Tales by Nina Simonds and Leslie Swartz. Age: 4-8. ISBN: 0152019839.
Lo and Behold: Good Enough to Eat by Benedict Norbert Wong. ISBN: 0972819215.
The Food and Cooking of China by Francine Halvorsen. ISBN: 0471110558.
Chinese Food and Folklore by Jeni Wright. ISBN: 1571456406.
Shark's Fin and Sichuan Pepper: A Sweet-Sour Memoir of Eating in China by Fuchsia Dunlop. ISBN: 0393066576.

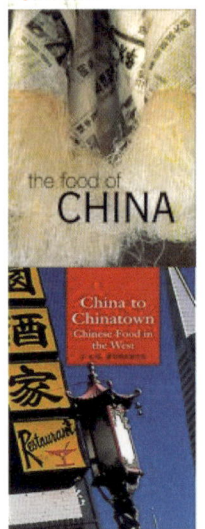

Cookbooks

The Science Chef Travels Around the World: Fun Food Experiments and Recipes for Kids by Joan D'Amico and Karen Eich Drummond. Age: 9-12. ISBN: 047111779X.
Fun with Asian Foods: A Kid's Cookbook by Devagi Sanmugum. Age: 9-12. ISBN: 0794603394.
The Young Chef's Chinese Cookbook by Frances Lee. Age: 9-12. ISBN: 0778702944.
The Food of China by Nina Simonds. ISBN: 1740452844.
The Everything Chinese Cookbook: From Wonton Soup to Sweet and Sour Pork by Rhonda Lauret Parkinson. ISBN: 1580629547.
Simple Chinese Cooking by Kylie Kwong. ISBN: 0670038482.
Land of Plenty: A Treasury of Authentic Sichuan Cooking by Fuchsia Dunlop. ISBN: 0393051773.
Beyond the Great Wall: Recipes and Travels in the Other China by Jeffrey Alford and Naomi Duquid. ISBN: 1579653014.
My Grandmother's Chinese Kitchen: 100 Family Recipes and Life Lessons by Eileen Yin-Fei Lo. ISBN: 1557885052.

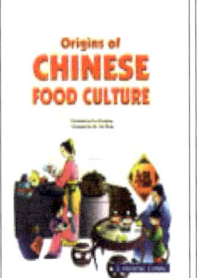 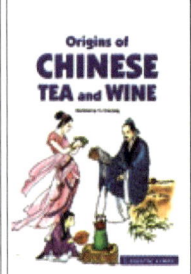  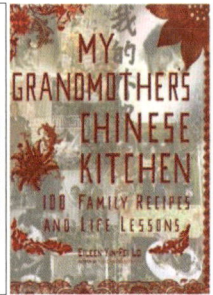   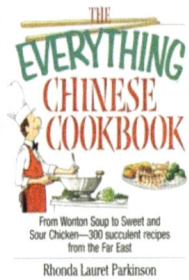

© Copyright 2009 - All rights reserved by OCDF Publications. Single classroom and single event use permitted for purchaser of book.